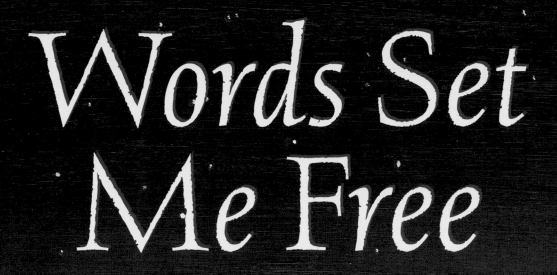

Words Set Me Free

THE STORY OF YOUNG
FREDERICK DOUGLASS

LESA CLINE-RANSOME

Illustrated by JAMES E. RANSOME

A Paula Wiseman Book

SIMON & SCHUSTER BOOKS FOR YOUNG READERS

New York   London   Toronto   Sydney

SIMON & SCHUSTER BOOKS FOR YOUNG READERS • An imprint of Simon & Schuster Children's Publishing Division • 1230 Avenue of the Americas, New York, New York 10020 • Text copyright © 2012 by Lesa Cline-Ransome • Illustrations copyright © 2012 by James E. Ransome • All rights reserved, including the right of reproduction in whole or in part in any form. • SIMON & SCHUSTER BOOKS FOR YOUNG READERS is a trademark of Simon & Schuster, Inc. • For information about special discounts for bulk purchases, please contact Simon & Schuster Special Sales at 1-866-506-1949 or business@simonandschuster.com. • The Simon & Schuster Speakers Bureau can bring authors to your live event. For more information or to book an event, contact the Simon & Schuster Speakers Bureau at 1-866-248-3049 or visit our website at www.simonspeakers.com. • Book design by Laurent Linn • The text for this book is set in Centaur. • The illustrations for this book are rendered in acrylic and oil paints. • Manufactured in China • 0923 SCP • 14 13 12 • Library of Congress Cataloging-in-Publication Data • Cline-Ransome, Lesa. • Words set me free : the story of young Frederick Douglass / Lesa Cline-Ransome ; illustrated by James E. Ransome. • p. cm. • "A Paula Wiseman book". • Summary: "Words Set Me Free is the inspiring story of young Frederick Douglass's path to freedom through reading"—Provided by publisher. • Includes bibliographical references and index. • ISBN 978-1-4169-5903-8 (hardcover) • 1. Douglass, Frederick, 1818–1895—Childhood and youth—Juvenile literature. 2. Slaves—United States—Biography—Juvenile literature. 3. Abolitionists—United States—Biography—Juvenile literature. 4. African American abolitionists—Biography—Juvenile literature. 5. Antislavery movements—United States—History—19th century—Juvenile literature. I. Ransome, James, ill. II. Title. • E449.D75C55 2012   973.8092—dc23   [B]   2011013323

All quotations are the words of Frederick Douglass and are taken from *The Narrative of the Life of Frederick Douglass*, which is sourced in the Bibliography of this book.

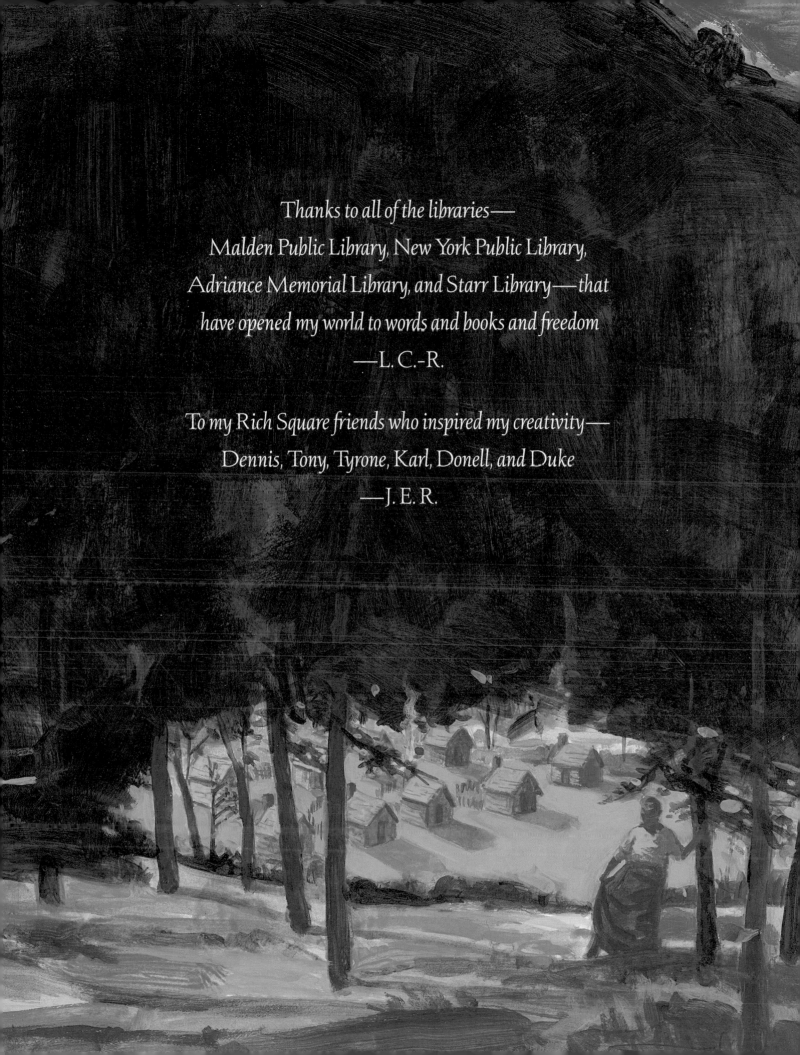

Thanks to all of the libraries—
Malden Public Library, New York Public Library,
Adriance Memorial Library, and Starr Library—that
have opened my world to words and books and freedom
—L. C.-R.

To my Rich Square friends who inspired my creativity—
Dennis, Tony, Tyrone, Karl, Donell, and Duke
—J. E. R.

My Mama was named Harriet Bailey. They say my master, Captain Aaron Anthony, was my daddy. After I was born, they sent me to my Grandmamma, and my Mama to another plantation. But, when she could, she'd walk the twelve miles in the middle of the night to come and see me. It must have been a long walk 'cause by the time she got there, she was too tired to talk. I remember she would just sit on the dirt floor near my pallet watching me. I never saw her face in the light of day. In the morning she'd be gone. Sometimes I wondered if I had only dreamed she was by my side, her rough hands gently stroking my face. When I was still young, Cook told me my Mama took sick. I never saw her again.

     I lived with my Grandmamma Betsey in her cabin until our master told her to bring me up to the big house on what we called Great House Farm. Grandmamma went back to her cabin, but I stayed behind with the other slave children. I was just six years old.

     Much of my time was my own as I was not yet old enough to work the fields. We ate our two meals a day out of a trough just like the animals in the barn. We were always hungry so we shoved down our meals of cornmeal mush with shells and dirty hands. But even the animals were rested in the heat of the afternoon sun, and they were never whipped bloody for being too tired or too sick or too slow.

At eight years old my mistress told me I was leaving the plantation to go to another master, her brother-in-law, in Baltimore. Master rented me out to make extra money. I could not imagine a life beyond my plantation. From Cousin Tom, an older slave on the plantation who had once been to Baltimore, he told me of a city so big and pretty, it seemed like a thousand Great House Farms.

On a Saturday when we sailed down the Miles River with all I owned in the world, my first pair of scratchy breeches and a shift, I did not cry. I was ready to leave Talbot County, Maryland, behind. We arrived at Smith's wharf on Sunday morning. Old Tom never told me that Baltimore looked as if it floated on a sea of waves.

At the Alliciana Street home of my new master, Hugh Auld, his wife,
Sophia, opened the door and greeted me. Missus was small, not much bigger
than me, and she had the first friendly white face I had ever seen.

It took us a while to get used to each other. She had never owned slaves and
I had never been treated like a paid servant. I was glad no one ever told her
that there is a big difference between a servant you pay and a slave you own.

During the day I ran errands for my master. In the evenings Missus sat by the fire and read her Bible aloud. Her kindly smile and voice warmed me as I entered the room. I do not know why, but I asked her to teach me to read.

On that night, she took me directly into her library, pulled out the first book she saw and sat me down next to her. We started with the letter *A* and she continued from there. The letters felt strange on my lips.

As I read, I remembered hearing of a boy, back on the plantation, who had his thumb chopped off when he was caught reading, and the letters I was reciting got caught in my throat.

I remembered my old master's words when he gathered all us slaves together to announce anyone caught trying to read will be whipped. And my mouth was dry.

Every day she gave me more letters to learn, until I knew I had the whole alphabet and a few words memorized.

She promised me that soon I would be able to read the Bible on my own. I wanted to read for myself where in the Bible it said one man should own another. But before that could happen, he found out.

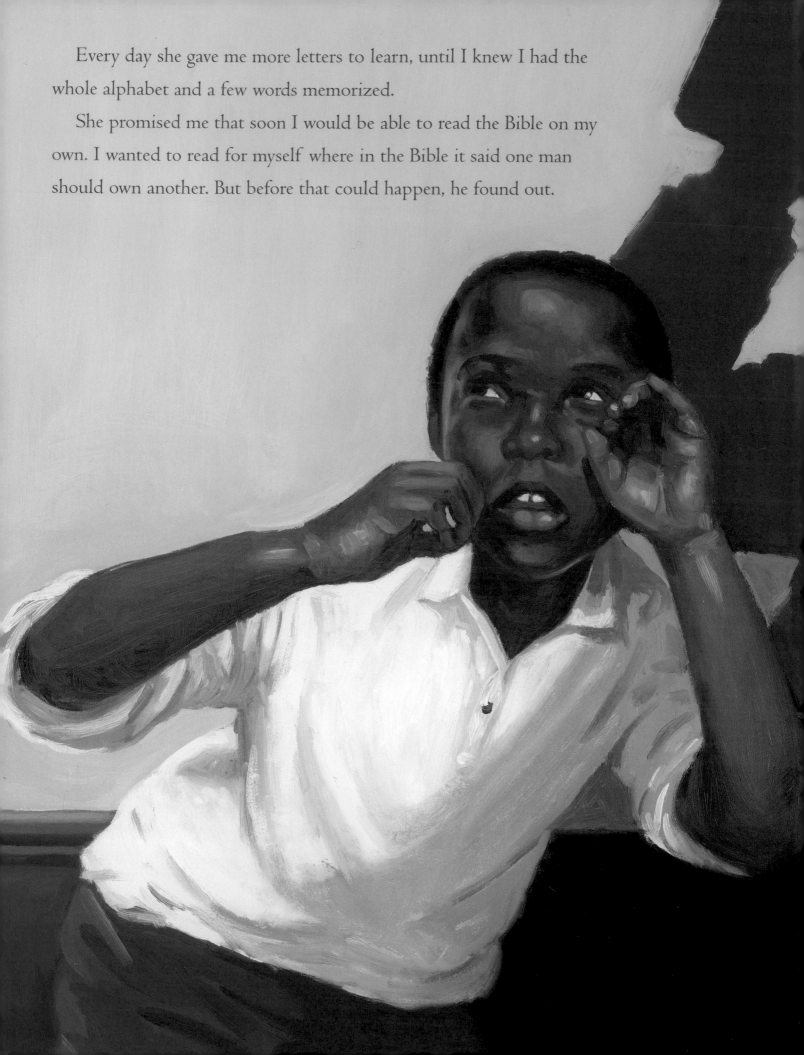

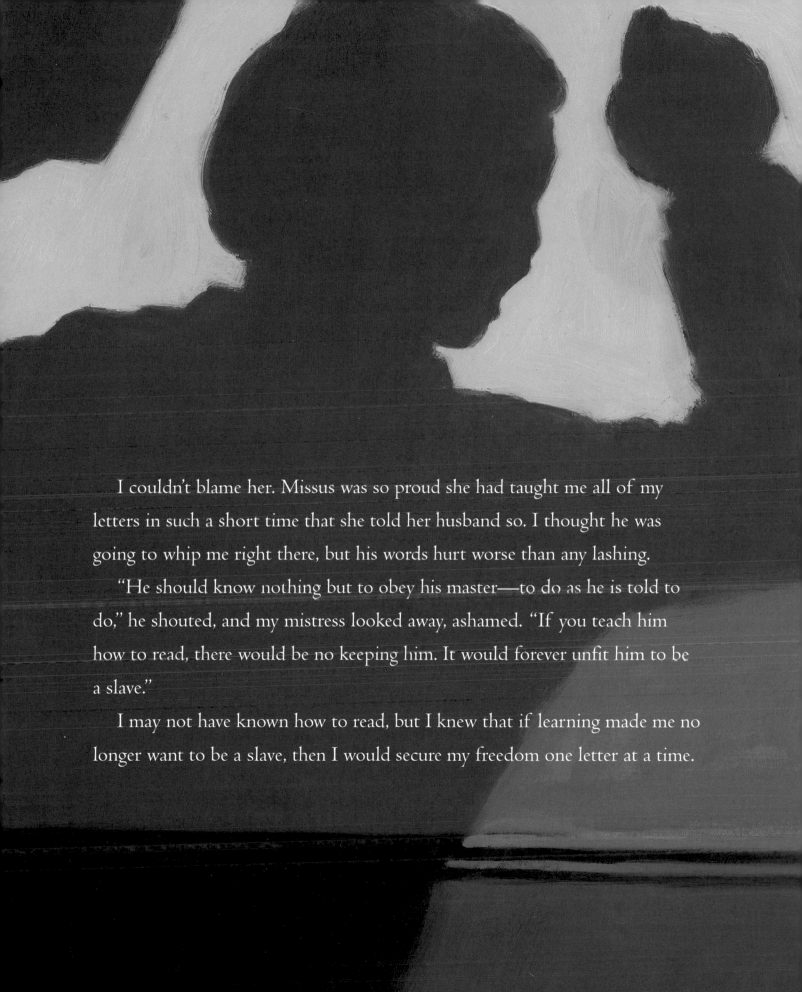

I couldn't blame her. Missus was so proud she had taught me all of my letters in such a short time that she told her husband so. I thought he was going to whip me right there, but his words hurt worse than any lashing.

"He should know nothing but to obey his master—to do as he is told to do," he shouted, and my mistress looked away, ashamed. "If you teach him how to read, there would be no keeping him. It would forever unfit him to be a slave."

I may not have known how to read, but I knew that if learning made me no longer want to be a slave, then I would secure my freedom one letter at a time.

She locked the door to the library and hid away the newspapers. She watched me all the time to make sure I was not putting together any more of those letters she had taught me. I knew she wished she could take it all back. But it was too late.

With a brick and a lump of chalk was first how I practiced my letters. Scratched them all along the bricked streets and wooden fences of Baltimore. *P* looked like a sail on one of the ships. *L* was a leg with a big foot. Two sticks crossed in the middle, that was *X*.

There was plenty of food in Master Auld's house. Food enough to share. I started bringing along some bread in case some of the white children from the neighborhood needed convincing. They did not have much, so for just a piece of bread I dared them to write letters better than me. What they wrote, I copied.

I told them my name. "Let me see you try it," I said.

Fast as I could, I ran to complete all my errands for my missus, then me and my new friends would get to work on my writing.

Rolled in the seat of my breeches was where I kept my copy book. Mine now that I took it from Master's son, Thomas. Even though he was only six, Missus said he learned his letters a year ago. He was reading now.

While I ran through the wharves and narrow streets of Baltimore, I was reading. The words the ship carpenters scribbled on timbers and masts, the names of shops and streets, headlines from the newspapers held in a newsboy's hand. I kept all those words in my head and copied them into my book when I got a chance.

As I ran I could almost feel myself free. Running to a home where no man called himself a master of another.

Sometimes, before I returned, I stood on the docks watching the ships, free to go as they pleased.

At twelve years old, with tips I saved from my errands, I bought my first newspaper and learned new words—*liberty, justice,* and *freedom. Abolition* was the word the newspapers used when they called for ending slavery. These were the words my master would never want me to see.

Now that I was reading about Negroes in the North, free from the burden of slavery, it was as if someone had lit a candle to my world. I saw freedom everywhere I looked, and the hope of it was what kept me alive.

For seven years I worked for my master and his missus down at the shipyard, lifting and laboring, and back at their house, toting and hauling— always pretending to be something I was not—content to be a slave.

When my old master, Captain Anthony, died, I had to return to Great House Farm to be divided up with the rest of his property, along with the sheep, the horses, and the swine.

Great House Farm remained the same. Hunger, weariness, and sadness seeped into the souls of every slave.

The boy who returned to his birthplace was not the same one who had left years earlier. That young boy was replaced with a fifteen-year-old who was free on the inside but not yet free on the outside.

Though my copy books and newspapers were long gone, words comforted

me in the fields as I chopped cotton from sunup to sundown. And words lay down with me at night, when my body ached with pain and hunger. I knew that the words would put an end to my suffering. I just wasn't sure when and how.

I was hired out to work for Mr. William Freeland, and while he was kinder than most, he was still a man who believed it was his divine right to own another human being.

Since my return to Talbot County, I became friends with Henry, John, and Handy, and I often spoke of my years in Baltimore. When I first told them I'd learned to read, they stopped short and looked around to see if anyone else was nearby.

They asked me to teach them. I did.

That's how I knew I could trust them.

From then on I thought I would devote "my Sundays to teaching these my loved fellow-slaves how to read."

At first we had school among the trees. Me scratching out letters and words in the dirt with a stick. John caught on fast and he helped me teach the others. They never missed a Sunday. Sometimes they brought others who then brought others. We had a school before long, but as far as the master knew, we were having church. Sitting on rocks and stumps and tired from the weeks' work, we sang out the alphabet like we sang out spirituals. Those of us who could, read from the Bible. We were doing God's work.

During one of our *services*, I got the idea for how I could run. Someone mentioned they knew where Master kept his paper and quills and did I think we could use them. At first I said no, we needed nothing from Master. But then I started thinking.

First I approached John, and then three others decided to join us in our escape. We would steal a boat from the neighboring Hamilton farm, and make our way in the night on the Chesapeake Bay. From there we would follow the North Star.

Eight years had passed since I sat in the library of Missus Auld learning my letters. And eight years still since Master Auld had issued the warning to his wife. It was the only time in my life when I agreed with my master. I was now unfit to be a slave.

Just before Easter, with a fine quill and paper secured by one of the house slaves, I wrote in a firm and steady hand,

This is to certify that I, the undersigned, to have given the bearer, my servant, Frederick Bailey, full liberty to go to Baltimore to spend the Easter Holidays. Written with mine own hand, &c., 1835

William Hamilton

Near St. Michael's, in Talbot county, Maryland.

I always knew that somehow words would set me free. But words on paper were now going to let me walk right out of Talbot County and into freedom up north.

AUTHOR'S NOTE

Frederick Bailey did not escape that evening. An informant revealed their plot to the master and all members in the party were jailed. Before he was taken away, Frederick managed to throw away his pass and instructed his friends to swallow the passes he had written for them, whispering, "Own nothing." After a week in prison and fearing he'd be killed if he stayed in the area, he was freed by his master and returned to Hugh Auld in Baltimore. Three years later, on September 3, 1838, Frederick, with the help of conductors on the Underground Railroad, successfully escaped to New York, where he changed his name to Frederick Douglass. He eventually moved to New Bedford, Massachusetts, with his wife, Anna Murray. Like most slaves, Frederick never knew his actual birth date, but when he was seventeen years old, his master estimated it to be February 1818.

In 1841 he was invited to speak at an Anti-Slavery Society meeting, and he became a lecturer on the abolition of slavery. In 1845 he wrote and published his first book, *Narrative of the Life of Frederick Douglass, an American Slave*, which described the evils of slavery, and it immediately became a bestseller. Two years later he began an abolitionist newspaper, *The North Star*.

BIBLIOGRAPHY

Douglass, Frederick. *Narrative of the Life of Frederick Douglass, an American Slave.* New York: Barnes & Noble Books, 2003.

Foner, Philip S. *The Life and Writings of Frederick Douglass: Early Years 1817–1849.* New York: International Publishers, 1950.

Frederick Douglass National Historic site. Accessed June 10, 2010. http://www.nps.gov/frdo/index.htm

Russell, Sharman Apt. *Frederick Douglass.* Danbury, Conn.: Chelsea House, 1988.

DOUGLASS TIMELINE

1818, Frederick is born near Easton, Maryland.

1824, six years old—Frederick's grandmother is forced to leave him to work with his siblings at the Lloyd Plantation (Great House Farm).

1825, seven years old—Frederick sees his mother for the last time, scolding a household cook who disliked Frederick. A few months later, his mother, Harriet, died. He would not learn of this until much later.

1826, eight years old—Frederick travels to Baltimore to work for Hugh Auld.

1833, fifteen years old—Frederick is sent to work near the Lloyd Plantation.

1834, sixteen years old—Frederick is sent to work nearby for Edward Covey.

1835, seventeen years old—Frederick is sent to work for William Freeland. Frederick started an illegal school and, with five other slaves, planned an escape. (Frederick wrote letters to protect them.) One of Frederick's associates exposed the escape group. They were captured and imprisoned. The Auld family came and released him. He went back to work for them as a ship caulker.

1838, twenty years old—Frederick escapes to New York.